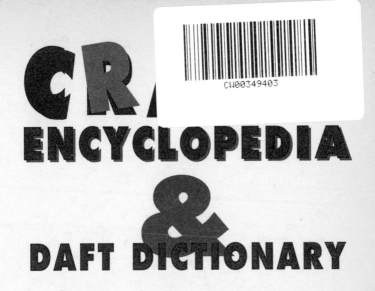

CRAZY ENCYCLOPEDIA & DAFT DICTIONARY

Gyles Brandreth

Illustrations by
Bobbie Craig
Ian West

CHANCELLOR
PRESS

Crazy Encyclopedia first published in 1981 by Carousel
Daft Dictionary first published in 1978 by Corgi-Carousel

This collected volume first published in 1995 by Chancellor Press
an imprint of Reed Consumer Books Limited
Michelin House, 81 Fulham Road, London SW3 6RB
and Auckland, Melbourne, Singapore and Toronto

ISBN: 1 85152 768 0

A CIP catalogue record is available from the British Library

Printed in Great Britain by Cox & Wyman Limited

CONTENTS

CRAZY
ENCYCLOPEDIA

CONTENTS

An encyclopaedia is not a bicycle but a book—a very special book that tells you everything you **never** needed to know. This one is particularly useless. Here's what's in it.

ANCIENT JOKES

These are the oldest jokes in the history of the world. They are also the worst. They have pride of place in the **Crazy Encyclopaedia** simply because they're so ancient and so awful they're sure to drive you **crazy**!

What is the proper name for a water otter?
A kettle.

What's a Hindu?
Lay eggs.

What did the simpleton call his pet tiger?
Spot.

Why do elephants eat camphor balls?
To keep the moths away from their trunks.

Why did the hatstand in the hall?
Because it had nowhere to sit.

What will the first clock on the moon be called?
A luna-tick.

How do you make a Swiss roll?
Push him over the Alps.

How do you get a baby astronaut to sleep?
You rock-et.

Which reptile is good at sums?
An Adder.

My brother is famous for his bird
impressions.
He eats worms.

**What is the best cure for water on
the brain?**
A tap on the head.

Did the butcher have
pigs' feet, Johnny?
I couldn't see, Mum—
he had his shoes on.

Doctor: You're OK, you'll live to be
70.
Patient: But I am 70.
Doctor: There, what did I tell you.

What does an elephant do when it rains?

Gets wet.

Two lions escaped from the zoo and decided to take a walk along the seafront at Blackpool. Said one: Not many people about for a Bank Holiday.

What would you call a man who owned all the cows in Arabia?

A Milk Sheikh.

'My dog has no nose.'
How does it smell?
'Terrible.'

9

Did you hear about the hedgehog who married a scrubbing brush?

And about the two rabbits who got married and went on a bunnymoon?

Doctor, about those tablets you gave me to build up my strength—well, I can't get the lid off the bottle.

How do you use an Egyptian doorbell?
Toot-and-come-in.

What did the vegetarian cannibal eat?
Swedes.

Did you hear about the Australian who made himself a new boomerang. And then went mad trying to throw the old one away.

Doctor: You need glasses
Patient: How do you know?
Doctor: I could tell as soon as you walked through the window.

Madam, your dog's been seen chasing a man on a bicycle.
Nonsense, Officer, my dog hasn't got a bicycle.

Seven tomatoes on a plate—which one was the cowboy?
None, they were all redskins.

How many kilometres can a pirate ship travel?
Ten kilometres to the galleon.

Waiter, be so good as to remove this fly from my soup.
Do it yourself, I'm not a lifeguard.

Molly: I've changed my mind.
Milly: Does it work any better?

Why did the ocean roar?
Because it had lobsters in its bed.

What can you make that no-one can see?
Noise.

Teacher: Where was the Magna Carta signed?
Pupil: At the bottom.

What are the largest ants in the world?
Elephants.

What is a cannibal's favourite soup?
One with plenty of body in it.

Which is the most expensive breed of dog?
The deerhound (dear hound).

1st Eskimo boy: Where does your mother come from?
2nd Eskimo boy: Alaska
1st Eskimo boy: Don't bother, I'll ask her myself.

Who was the greatest King never crowned?
King Kong.

Why do bakers work so hard?
Because they knead the dough.

Why do bees hum?
Because they don't know the words.

Why was Lassie a famous dog in films?
Because she was always given the lead.

Johnny: Dad, what's got a purple-spotted body, great hairy legs and bulging eyes?
Dad: I don't know, why?
Johnny: Well, there's one crawling up your trouser leg.

On-looker: Is this river good for fish?

Fisherman: It must be. I can't get any to leave it.

How did Little Bo Peep lose her sheep?

She had a crook with her.

What's the best cure for water on the knees?

Drainpipe trousers.

Where do parrots go to take their A-levels?

To a polly-technic.

If buttercups are yellow, what colour are hiccups?

Burple.

15

Why was the sheep arrested on the motorway?
Because it made a ewe turn.

What has a neck but can't swallow?
A bottle.

Where will you find a stuffed cow?
In the Natural history Mooseum.

What is 333 metres high, French and wet?
The Eiffel Shower.

Which sea do spaceships sail on?
The Galaxy.

When does a fire flare up?
When it is bellowed at.

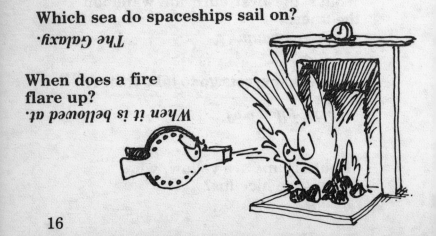

Teacher: This essay on 'My Dog' is word for word the same as your sister's.
Pupil: I know, sir, it's the same dog.

Policeman: Did you know your wife fell out of the car a few kilometres back.
Motorist: Thank God for that, I thought I'd gone deaf.

Who wrote Great Eggspectations?
Charles Chickens.

Customer: Those mothballs you sold me are no good.
Shopkeeper: Why's that?
Customer: I haven't hit a single moth with them yet.

What's black, dangerous and hides in trees?
A crow with a sub-machine gun.

Waiter, there's a twig in my soup. Just a moment, sir, I'll fetch the branch manager.

How do you rob ice-cream vans?
Stick 'em up and grab the lolly.

What do cats read every morning?
Mewspapers.

What do you call a highwayman with flu?
Sick Turpin.

What would you call a bald Grizzly?
Fred Bear.

Joe: What's the best way to catch a rabbit?
Jim: Hide behind a bush and make a noise like a lettuce.

What can you hold without touching it?
Your breath.

Did you hear about the Magician whose favourite trick was to saw a woman in half?
She's in hospital now, in Wards 7 and 8.

What's the difference between lightning and electricity?
Did you ever get a lightning bill?

Suzie: I know the score of any game before it starts.
Sally: Any game? Give me an example.
Suzie: Nil—Nil!

What has pretty wings, sits on flowers and is deadly?
A man-eating butterfly.

Eccentric old lady: I'd like a pair of crocodile shoes.
Shop Assistant: What size does your crocodile take?

What did the zoo keeper see when the elephant squirted water from his trunk?
A jumbo jet.

Mum: Shall I put the kettle on?
Dad: No, dear, it wouldn't suit you.

Who invented the first pen?
The Incas (Inkers).

What prize did the man who invented the doorknocker win?
The Nobel Prize.

What do snowmen dance at?
A snowball.

How do you make a sausage roll?
Push it.

Teacher: I wish you'd pay a little attention.
Pupil: I'm paying as little as I can.

Why don't elephants eat penguins?
Because they can't get the wrappers off.

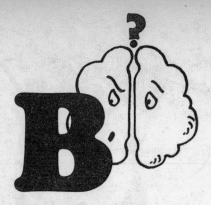

BRAIN BOGGLERS

The Crazy Encyclopaedia proudly presents some brainteasing mindbenders that will really get your senses reeling. For every mind boggler you manage to complete in under an hour, score ten marks. A total score of 20 or more is impressive. 30 or more suggests you're a genius. 40 or more proves you cheated. Good luck.

1. Without taking your pencil off the page, can you connect these dots to form a triangle?

2. Which of the two lines is longer? (Go carefully here—your eyes may fool you.)

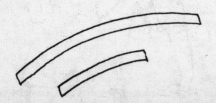

3. Can you spot the odd man out in this series?

4. Can you get the dog to the bone in this amazing maze?

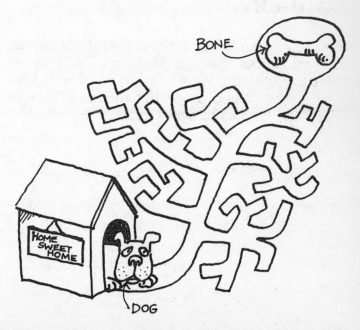

(You will find the answers on page 129.)

COOKERY

Welcome to the **Crazy Encyclopaedia's** unique cookery course. Eat our food and you'll never want to eat again. Here are our three most popular dishes. When preparing them, be sure to follow the recipes in every detail.

CROC AU VIN

28 PEPPERCORNS

Ingredients:
two old crocodile-skin handbags, or
a pair of snakeskin shoes
½ bottle of red wine (Burpundy is
best, but if you can't get it, try Bore-
deau.)
28 black peppercorns
three used sticking-plasters
a daffodil bulb.

Method: Peel and chop the daffodil bulb
(and probably your finger). Crush the peppercorns (and probably your finger). Go to
hospital and get your finger fixed. Come
home and beat the handbag and shoes with
a meat-tenderising hammer. Then cook the
lot in a deep saucepan on a low heat for 117
hours. Serve on a bed of nails, garnished
with varnish.

A SPECIAL CAKE FOR WHEN YOUR HEAD TEACHER RETIRES
DUNCANIN CAKE

Ingredients:
> 3 old canes, chopped
> 12 French text books, shredded
> ½ and old shoebag, minced
> one gallon best school custard
> the dinner-lady's hairnet
> some floor-sweepings from woodwork

Method: Put all the ingredients together in a big bowl. Stir continuously, adding rotten eggs till a) you faint b) the mixture reaches the right constituency. (If you don't know what the right constituency is, telephone your MP). Then turn the mixture out into a greased waste-bin and leave it to balance on top of the Head's door. He'll be touched.

TOAD IN THE HOLE

Ingredients:
A toad
A hole

Method: Well, we were going to give details of this traditional British dish but we've heard that it's still Top Secret. So alas, the **method** section has had to be censored. But perhaps you'd like to think of all the things you could do with a toad and a hole and you might stumble on it. (If you stumble upon the toad, by the way—watch out! They can turn nasty when roused).

The **Crazy Encyclopaedia** is nothing if not international, so now we are proud to present the very best in Australian **haute cuisine**. Australian cooking uses the region's own wonderful natural products: wombats, cricket bats, boomerangs, and above all The Bush. (Vegetarians are well catered for with Bush Salad, Bushatouille, Curried Bush and Bush and Chips.)

27

So why don't you horrify your friends with an unusual meal of **ROAST LEG OF KANGAROO, WOLLAMOGGA STYLE**.

First, catch your Kangaroo. There are several sure-fire methods: the flying tackle, the flying doctor, the block-and-tackle, the blockbuster—or you may find that a carrot on the end of a piece of string works wonders.

Once you've got the Kangaroo's leg ready for roasting, you'll find your oven's much too small as most Kangaroos' legs are nearly 2 metres long!

D

DAFFYDUCK

DAFFYNITIONS

For really daffy daffynitions you need a copy of
Gyles Brandreth's classic work of reference **The
Daft Dictionary** (a Carousel paperback available at all the best bookshops), but to give you
an idea of what it's all about here are a handful
of crazy definitions which, as you will see, give
ordinary words quite extraordinary meanings.

Grandson: A good boy
Myth: A female moth

Selfish: What fishmongers do

29

Fireplace: A shooting range
Handicap: Useful hat
Minimum: A very small mother
Intense: Where campers sleep

Barbecue: People waiting to have their hair cut

Adore: Something you walk through
Knapsack: A sleeping bag
Bouyant: Brother of a sister ant
Hatchet: What a bird tries to do when it sits on an egg

Snoring:	Sheet music
Pigeon-toed:	Half pigeon, half toad
Aperitif:	A pair of French false teeth
Dandelion:	A well dressed lion

Kernel:	The rank above a Major
Nightmare:	A dark horse
Legend:	A foot
Extinct:	The smell of bad eggs
Onward:	Where a nurse works
Draughtsman:	Someone who leaves doors open
Acorn:	What you get through wearing tight shoes
Addition:	What a dining table has (a dish on)

31

Jamaica:	4,840 square metres of jam
Amidst:	A thick fog
Angel:	A heavenly creature that is always harping on something or other.
Asian flu:	Part of a Chinese chimney.
Atlas:	The greatest thief in history. He held up the whole world.
Bachelor:	A man who never Mrs. anybody.
Friday:	The best day of the week for frying
Guerilla warfare:	Monkeys throwing coconuts at each other
Leopard:	A spotted lion

Pig:	An animal that has to be killed in order to be cured.
Rhubarb:	Celery with sunburn

Robin:	A bird that steals
Horseman:	Someone who is half horse and half man
Undercover Agent:	A spy in bed.

ENGINEERING

Engineering is a serious business—except when you have a copy of the **Crazy Encyclopaedia** beside you and you can learn all about **crazy** engineering and so make yourself a **crazy** friend: a riotous, rollicking robot specially programmed to make you laugh—and do the housework! Here it is:

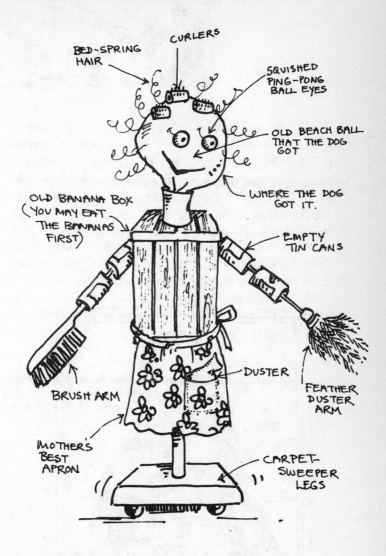

CURLERS

BED-SPRING HAIR

SQUISHED PING-PONG BALL EYES

OLD BEACH BALL THAT THE DOG GOT

WHERE THE DOG GOT IT.

OLD BANANA BOX (YOU MAY EAT THE BANANAS FIRST)

EMPTY TIN CANS

DUSTER

BRUSH ARM

FEATHER DUSTER ARM

MOTHER'S BEST APRON

CARPET-SWEEPER LEGS

35

FINE ART

No encyclopaedia would be complete without a reproduction of the world's most famous painting, **The Mona Lisa**, by Leonardo da Vinci. Here it is—and as you will see restoration work (undertaken by the publishers of the **Crazy Encyclopaedia** at considerable expense) reveals that Lisa wasn't such a moaner after all.

We have restored a number of history's greatest works of art. Our most recent undertaking was the famous statue of the Greek God Zeus. For more than two thousand years it was thought that this was a statue of Zeus pondering:

As you will see on the next page, restoration shows it's actually a statue of Zeus reading a book by Gyles Brandreth:

The book reads:
1000
RIDDLES
TO
GREA...
RIDDLES
EVER
KNOWN
GYLES BRANDRETH

GHOSTS

You may have heard the expression 'to give up the ghost' but you probably have not known how to get hold of a ghost in order to be able to give it up. Well, your problem is solved. The publishers of the **Crazy Encyclopaedia** have recently launched the **RUSTY CHAIN MAIL ORDER SCHEME**, so that you can now buy a ghost through the post.

All you have to do is flick through this catalogue and pick the spook of your choice—but hurry while stocks last.

SIR LANCELOT HORRID-THYNGGE OF HEADLESSE HALL

Sir Lancelot comes gift-wrapped. When unwrapped he is revealed in all his glory: a genuine Elizabethan ghost, who will still fit in to any other decor very well and bring an aristocratic air to your home.

He walks, he talks, he drips blood (or if you're worried about the carpets, order the special water-dripping variety).

SPECIAL FEATURES

Detachable head for easy cleaning. When not wanted, he easily fades away into the nearest wall. Good Educational value for children studying the Elizabethan Age. An excellent "congratulations" present for when your child gets ahead at school.

PRICE: £36.50 plus VAT of Malmsey

MAD NED BELLY, THE ONE-EYED CONVICT

Mad Ned is available in a choice of colours: slime green, toad brown or spit grey. Choose one to match your colour scheme. Ned will scrabble madly at the walls, dribble madly down the curtains, and swear loudly in the cupboard. For this reason he might not be a very suitable present for old ladies (for them, we suggest the peaceful and house-trained Drowned Lass of MacOctopus Hall—see below.)

SPECIAL FEATURES
Mad Ned's most special feature is his one

eye. He can make it materialise at will wherever he wants it to—on top of your Christmas tree, for example. Or in the middle of nasty Cousin Eric's plate of eggs and bacon.

Another Special Feature is Ned's Ball and Chain. It comes in easy-care **RUSTY CAST IRON** and on nights when the moon is full it can go flying through the air, wall, or colour TV screen. On ordinary nights he just drags it up and down on the landing.

> **PRICE:** £40.99 or £60.99 for Gold-Plated Ball and Chain and special flashing tooth.

THE DROWNED LASS OF MACOCTOPUS HALL

Rumoured to be Teenie Jeannie, the daughter of the Laird, this small figure is especially suitable for old ladies or people who live in small flats, as she is quiet, docile and well-behaved. It's rumoured that Jeannie fell in love with the infamous Haggis-Snatcher Fergus MacKnee, and that when her father forbade the match she drowned herself in Loch Jaw.

£25.99

SPECIAL FEATURES

She weeps, she wails, she wrings her hands—
and anything else she can lay her hands on.
So she can be a great help around the house,
being easily trained to wring the washing,
etc.

Jeannie is a drip-dry ghost—or at least,
she's drip-wet (because of the drowning, you
see.) So when the carpets are absolutely
soaking, it's best to hang her up on a clothes-
hanger above the bath and ask her to wring
herself out. When she's done so, she will
obligingly disappear down the plughole.
She will eventually reappear—through the
bathroom ventilator, probably.

PRICE: £25.99 (Wet Suit £15 extra)

SPECIAL OFFER: SELF-ASSEMBLY GHOST

For the unbelievably low price of £12.99 we are able to offer a special self-assembly ghost. You receive a parcel of ghost fragments and put them together yourself with a few bolts and a ghouldriver.

A SAMPLE PACK SHOULD CONTAIN:

Screaming skull (state whether stereo or mono)

Neck Bolt

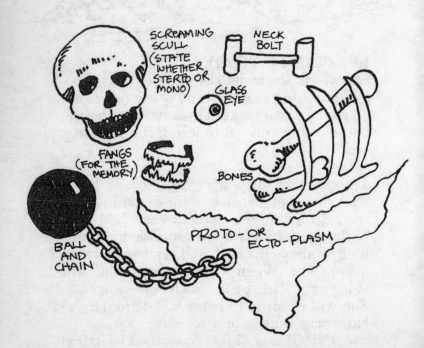

Glass Eye

Fangs (for the memory)

Blood

Bones

Ball & Chain

Proto- or Ecto-plasm

MONEY BACK IF NOT AFFRIGHTED

HOWLERS

You will have heard of 'schoolboy and schoolgirl howlers'. Here are ten of them:

Brussels is famous for sprouts and carpets

Noah's wife was Joan of Arc

Eskimos are God's frozen people.

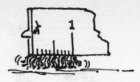

A centimetre is an insect with a hundred legs.

Imports are ports that are far inland.

I avenue baby sister.

She wanted to go butter mother wouldn't let her.

My brother and me hate washing in arrears.

Children should always show proper respect folder people.

These 'howlers' are silly mistakes that children are supposed to make at school. We wanted to publish ten pages of them, but having searched and searched and searched and **SEARCHED** and **SEARCHED** and only come up with a total of ten, we realised the truth of the matter: **CHILDREN NEVER MAKE SILLY MISTAKES AT SCHOOL.**

IGNORANCE

Ignorance is what you don't know and since what we don't know we don't know, we don't know what to put in this chapter.

We don't want to show you our ignorance, but some people aren't so shy. Walk down any street nowadays and look into any shop window and you'll see **'For Sale'** notices as ignorant as it is possible to be. These signs are fine examples of ignorance—and every one of them is real.

BULL DOG FOR SALE:
EATS ANYTHING. VERY FOND OF CHILDREN

FOR SALE: COMPLETE MAHOGNAY CHIP AND DALE DINING ROOM SET – IN GOOD CONDITION

FOR SALE: WOODEN ROCKING HORSE SUITABLE FOR CHILDREN WITH GREY SPOTS

49

GUITARS FOR SALE:
CHEAP, NO STRINGS ATTACHED.

cheap cheep
cheep cheep

TWO CANARIES FOR SALE:
CHEEP, CHEEP!

FOR SALE : LARGE CRYSTAL VASE
BY LADY SLIGHTLY CRACKED.

SILVER RINGS FOR SALE: ORDER YOUR RING BY POST. STATE SIZE AND SEND STRING TIED ROUND FINGER.

SCRAP CARS FOR SALE FIRST - CRASH CONDITION

DOCTOR'S SAILING BOAT PLUS ACCESORIES - DOCTOR NO FURTHER USE.

JOKES

These jokes aren't as old as the Ancient Jokes at the beginning of the book, but they're just as bad. In fact, some of them are worse.

Doctor, doctor, I feel like a dog.
Sit down and tell me about it.
I'm not allowed on the furniture.

What is a vampire's favourite fruit?
A blood orange.

If an Eskimo mum had a boy and a girl what would they be?
Blubber and sister.

What do you get if you cross a pig with the M1.
A road hog.

What is an Ig?
An Eskimo's house without a Loo.

52

What do hedgehogs have with their cheese?
Prickled onions.

What do geese eat?
Gooseberries.

Why is Rugby like a loaf of bread?
Because of its scrums (crumbs).

Policeman: (to motorist) I say, I say, I say, you've got a bald tyre there.
Motorist: Okay, officer, I'll see it gets some 'air.

What is soft, sweet, pink and white and comes from Mars?
Martian mallow.

Tommy: Is your dog a watch-dog?
Timmy: Yes.
Tommy: Ask him to tell me the time then.

What language do twins born in Holland speak?
Double-Dutch.

I've been trying to think of a word for about two weeks.
How about 'fortnight'!

What did one ear say to the other ear?
Between you and me we need a haircut.

Jack: I've lost my cat.
Jill: Why don't you put an ad in the paper?
Jack: Don't be silly, he can't read.

What is the largest species of mouse in the world?
Hippopotomouse.

Why did the farmer call his rooster Robinson?

Because he Crusoe.

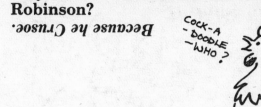

Naval Officer: Can you swim?
Cadet: Why have you run out of ships?

What would you get if you rang 666?

The fire brigade upside down.

What did one arithmetic book say to the other?

I've got a bit of a problem.

Patient: Doctor, can you help me out?
Doctor: Certainly, which way did you come in?

Where does an American Cow come from?

Moo York.

55

Where do elves go shopping?
To British Gnome Stores.

Where does Tarzan get his clothes?
From a jungle sale.

Doctor: You'll have to take things quietly.
Patient: I already do, I'm a burglar.

Why do bees have sticky hair?
Because they have honey combs.

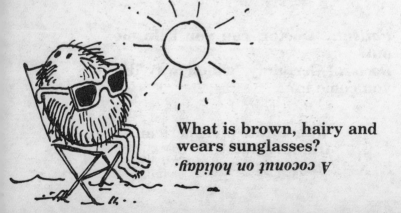

What is brown, hairy and wears sunglasses?
A coconut on holiday.

What is white outside, red inside and loved by birds?

A worm sandwich.

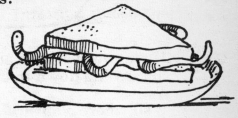

Did you hear about the man who stole some rhubarb?

He was put into custardy.

Doctor, doctor, everyone thinks I'm a liar!
I don't believe you.

Why is it dangerous to play cards in the jungle?

Because there are so many cheetahs.

Have you ever seen an elephant hiding upside down in custard?
No.
Well, there you are. It just shows what a good disguise custard is.

Where do astronauts leave their space ships?
At parking meteors.

Doctor: Do you have trouble in making up your mind?
Patient: Well, yes and no.

Pupil: I'm sorry I'm late sir, I sprained my ankle.
Teacher: Bah, another lame excuse.

Why were seven wooden planks standing in a circle?
They were having a board meeting.

What do you get if you plant an electric light bulb in space?
A rocket from the Electricity Board.

What turned the moon pale?
The At-mos-fear.

What do you get if you cross a cat with a ball of wool?
Mittens.

If a dog loses his tail, where does he go to get a new one?
To a re-tail shop.

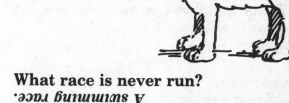

What race is never run?
A swimming race.

How does an intruder get into a house?
Intruder window.

Doctor, doctor, I keep thinking I'm a pound note.
Well, go shopping, the change'll do you good.

The judge found the blacksmith guilty of forging.

What is an octopus?
An eight-sided cat.

What's green and goes boing, boing, boing?
A spring cabbage.

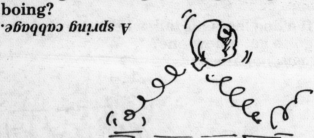

Which side has a chicken got the most feathers?
On the outside.

Customer: Waiter, there is a fly in this ice-cream.
Waiter: Serves him right, let him freeze.

What travels around the world but stays in a corner?
A stamp.

What can a bird do that a man cannot do?
Take a bath in a saucer.

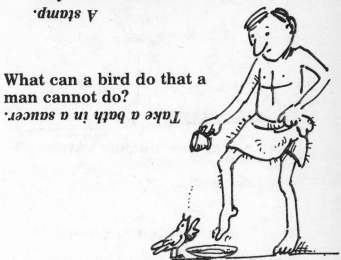

Simpleton: I wonder how long a person can live without a brain?
Simon: Well, how old are you?

Doctor: And what's the matter with you?
Patient: I've just swallowed a roll of film.
Doctor: Don't worry, nothing serious will develop.

What nationality is Santa Claus?
North Polish, I think.

What newspaper did the cavemen read?
The Prehistoric Times.

What kind of spy hangs around department stores?
A counterspy.

What age is most important to a car?
Mileage.

What vegetable needs a plumber?
A leek.

Did you hear about the fight on the train?
Yes. The inspector punched a ticket.

What's a howling baby whale?
A little blubber.

Why did the girl put her bed in the fireplace?

Because she wanted to sleep like a log.

What goes clomp, clomp, clomp, swish?

An elephant with wet plimsolls.

Why did the cookie cry?

Because its mother had been a wafer so long.

What is the difference between an angry audience and a cow with laryngitis?

One boos madly, the other moos badly.

Wife: How do you like the socks I mended?
Husband: They're darned good.

KNOCK KNOCKS

In the hope that Gyles Brandreth will soon be awarded the No-Bell Prize for Literature his **Crazy Encyclopaedia** now presents the thirty-five finest knock-knock jokes ever known. All you need to enjoy these to the full are a door and a door-knocker—and if you haven't got a door-knocker a hammer will do.

Knock, Knock

Knock, knock,
Who's there?
Ken.
Ken who?
Ken I come in?

Knock, knock,
Who's there?
Kanga,
Kanga who?
No, Kangaroo.

Knock, knock,
Who's there,
Amos,
Amos who?
A mosquito.

Knock, knock,
Who's there?
Arfer,
Arfer who?
Arfer got.

Knock, knock,
Who's there?
Justin,
Justin who?
Justin time for tea.

Knock, knock,
Who's there?
Arthur,
Arthur who,
Arthur any more sweets left?

Knock, knock,
Who's there?
You're a lady,
You're a lady who?
I didn't know you could yodel.

Knock, knock,
Who's there?
The invisible man,
Well, tell him I can't see him.

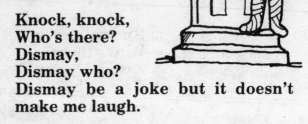

Knock, knock,
Who's there?
Dismay,
Dismay who?
Dismay be a joke but it doesn't make me laugh.

Knock, knock,
Who's there?
Alec,
Alec who?
Alec a nice cup of tea in the morning.

Knock, knock,
Who's there?
Police,
Police who?
Police let me in.

Knock, knock,
Who's there?
Willoughby,
Willoughby who?
Willoughby quick and let me in.

Knock, knock,
Who's there?
Isabel
Isabel who?
Isabel necessary on a bicycle?

Knock, knock,
Who's there?
Harriet,
Harriet who?
Harriet the last of the
sausages.

Knock, knock,
Who's there?
Sarah,
Sarah who?
Sarah doctor in the
house?

Knock, knock,
Who's there?
Author,
Author who?
Author any more at home
like you?

67

Knock, knock,
Who's there?
You,
You who?
Did you call?

Knock, knock,
Who's there?
A man who can't reach the bell.

Knock, knock,
Who's there?
Ivor,
Ivor who?
Ivor a good mind not to tell you.

Knock, knock,
Who's there?
Godfrey,
Godfrey who?
Godfrey tickets for the show.

Knock, knock,
Who's there?
Noah,
Noah who?
Noah good place to eat?

Knock, knock,
Who's there?
Jupiter,
Jupiter who?
Jupiter hurry or you'll miss the bus.

Knock, knock,
Who's there?
Aries,
Aries who?
Aries a Tavern in the town, in the
town....

Knock, knock,
Who's there?
Cook,
Cook who?
That's the first one I've heard this
year.

Knock, knock,
Who's there?
Europe,
Europe who?
Europe early this morning.

Knock, knock,
Who's there?
Boo,
Boo who?
Oh, don't start crying again.

Knock, knock,
Who's there?
Theresa,
Theresa who?
Theresa green—until the autumn.

Knock, knock,
Who's there?
Thistle,
Thistle who?
Thistle be the last time I knock on
your door.

Knock, knock,
Who's there?
Martini,
Martini who?
Martini hands are
frozen.

Knock, knock,
Who's there?
Irish stew,
Irish stew who?
Irish stew in the
name of the law!

Knock, knock,
Who's there?
Olive,
Olive who?
Olive here, so let me in.

Knock, knock,
Who's there?
Luke,
Luke who?
Luke through the keyhole and you'll
see.

Knock, knock,
Who's there?
Alison,
Alison who?
Alison Wonderland.

Knock, knock,
Who's there?
Ivor,
Ivor who?
Ivor a message for you.

Knock, knock,
Who's there?
Mary,
Mary who?
Mary in haste,
repent at leisure!

LOVE

In Volume Two of the **Crazy Encyclopaedia**, under S for Science, you will learn that it is love that makes the world go round. In this volume, under L for Love, you will learn how to make the world's most original **Valentine** cards.

A VALENTINE FOR THE GIRL WHO THINKS SHE'S THE MOST BEAUTIFUL THING SINCE FARRAH FAWCETT

YOU'RE SO BEAUTIFUL, SO PRECIOUS, SO RARE—

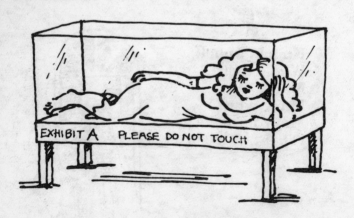

EXHIBIT A   PLEASE DO NOT TOUCH

YOU SHOULD BE LOCKED UP IN A MUSEUM!

FOR A BOY OR GIRL WHO FANCIES THEMSELVES
YOU'VE BROKEN SO MANY HEARTS ALREADY...

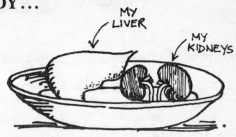

I THOUGHT I'D SEND YOU MY LIVER AND KIDNEYS INSTEAD

FOR A GUY WHO RECKONS HE'S TOUGH
YOU'RE SO MANLY, MUSCULAR AND STRONG...

WHY DON'T YOU TEAR YOURSELF IN HALF?

MUSIC

Let's start this chapter on a high note:

And let's continue it with some of the most melodious musical jokes of all:

Why is a piano like an eye?
Because they are both closed when their lids are down.

What's soft and yellow and goes round and round?
A long playing omelette.

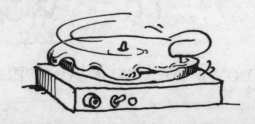

What has eight feet and can sing?
A quartet.

What brass instrument is like a potato?
A tuba.

What happened when the electric guitar was plugged into the lamp standard?
It played light music.

When is water musical?
When it's piping hot.

What is musical and holds 36 litres of beer?
A barrel organ.

Jimmy: I can sing 'Over the green hills and far away.'
Johnny: Well, the further away the better.

If pop music went metric would Mick Jagger sing with the Rolling Kilos?

Who is green, curly and musical?
Elvis Parsley.

What is creepy and plays the top twenty?
Tranny by Gaslight.

What is fat, musical and makes chips?
Tubby the tuba.

What do you call it when a symphony orchestra holds up a bank?
Robbery with violins.

Which members of an orchestra can't you trust?
The fiddlers.

What is romantic, musical and useful in a supermarket?
A Chopin Liszt.

Why did you give up tap dancing?
Because I kept falling in the sink.

What is sneezy, shocking and plays pop music?
An electric catarrh.

Did you hear about the musical thief?
He got away with the lute.

What is the difference between a fish and a piano?
You can't tuna fish.

77

N

THE ARTIST DIDN'T KNOW MUCH, SHE DIDN'T KNOW WHAT TO DRAW FOR N.? ?? ?? ??

NOLEDGE

How much do you no? Not enough? Well, don't worry, the **Crazy Encyclopaedia** is here to help. If you want to learn something new, you've come to the right place, because we've got information here that will amaze you. Some of it may be hard to believe—it is certainly hard to spell—but every word of it is true.

DID YOU NO THAT—

— **the elephant is the only animal to have four knees**

1 2 3 4

— **it is impossible to sneeze with your eyes open**

— **a fly's wings vibrate 340 times a second**

— **the maximum recorded life in years of a budgerigar is 28 years**

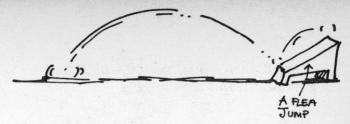

A FLEA JUMP

— a flea can jump 200 times its own length

— you blink 25 times every minute

— a hippopotamus can run faster than a man

— ice-cream was invented by a Frenchman called Gerald Tissain in 1620

— dogs sweat through their paws

— turtles have no teeth

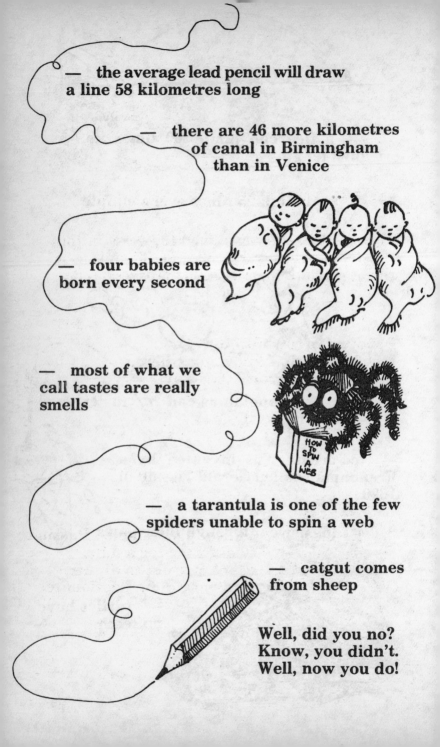

— the average lead pencil will draw a line 58 kilometres long

— there are 46 more kilometres of canal in Birmingham than in Venice

— four babies are born every second

— most of what we call tastes are really smells

— a tarantula is one of the few spiders unable to spin a web

— catgut comes from sheep

Well, did you no?
Know, you didn't.
Well, now you do!

ODES AND ENDS

There is no verse worse than the verse in this chapter: a truly crazy collection of ridiculous rhymes, lunatic limericks and the oddest of odes.

I shot an arrow into the air,
It fell to earth, I know not where,
I lose all my arrows that way.

I know a girl named Passion.
I asked for for a date,
I took her out to dinner,
And wow! how Passionate.

It doesn't breathe, it doesn't smell,
It doesn't feel so very well,
I am disgusted with my nose,
The only thing it does is blows.

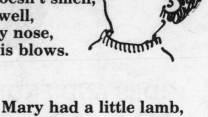

Mary had a little lamb,
Freddie had a pup,
Johnnie had a crocodile
It ate the others up.

My love is like a cabbage,
Divided into two,
The leaves I give to others
But the heart I give to you.

Some folks say that fleas are black,
But I know that's not so,
'Cause Mary had a little lamb'
With fleas as white as snow.

A
HEAVY
GRASSHOPPER

Way down South, where bananas
grow,
A grass hopper stepped on an
elephant's toe,
The elephant said, with tears in his
eyes,
'Pick on somebody your own size.'

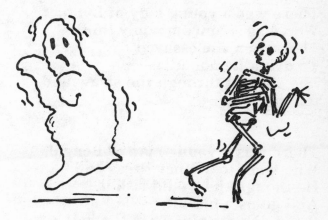

A skeleton once in Khartoum,
Invited a ghost to his room;
They spent the whole night
In a terrible fright
As to which should be frightened
of whom.

There was a young lady of Lynn,
Who was so uncommonly thin,
That when she essayed
To drink Lemonade,
She slipped through the straw and
fell in.

There was a young man of Bengal,
Who went to a fancy dress ball,
He thought he would risk it,
And go as a biscuit,
But a dog ate him up in the hall.

The Wonderful Wizard of Oz,
Retired from business because,
What with up-to-date science,
To most of his clients,
He wasn't the Wiz that he Woz.

PAPERBACKS

If you have enjoyed this book, you will want to buy Gyles Brandreth's other books. You will find a list of titles on page 2. When you have read and digested all his work—and some of the books are printed on rice paper to make the digestion easier—the **Crazy Encyclopaedia** recommends a visit to your local library or bookshop where you should do your best to get hold of one or two of these all-time classics, now reissued as paperbacks.

MAKE A PIG OF YOURSELF BY CHRIS. P. BACON

END OF THE WEEK BY GLADYS FRIDAY

WHO SAW HIM LEAVE BY WENDY GO

SAHARA JOURNEY BY I. RHODA CAMEL

SAYING YOUR PRAYERS - BY NEIL DOWN

ROUND THE MOUNTAIN BY SHEILA . B. CUMMING

OVER THE CLIFF - HUGO FIRST

DETECTIVE STORIES BY WATTS . E . DUNN

THE DOGS DINNER BY NORA BONE

FITTING CARPETS BY WALTER WALL

THE WINNER BY VIC TREE

EAGER GIRL BY MAY. I. HELP

THE PAINTER BY R.T. STICK

THE BROKEN WINDOW BY EVA BRICK

THE OPEN WINDOW BY EILEEN DOUBT

GHOST OF A LAYD — BY SHEILA PEER

BANBURY CROSS BY RHODA WHITEHORSE

THE OPEN GATE BY WANDA OFF

RAINCOATS BY ANNA RACK

HOW TO MAKE AN IGLOO BY S.K. MOW

HORSE RIDING EVENTS BY JIM KARNA

NECK EXERCISES BY G. RAFF

GUNFIRE BY R. TILLERY

THERE'S A HOLE IN MY BUCKET — LEE KING

THE OLYMPICS — BY ARTHUR LECTIC

A BAD REPORT — BY A. PAULINE WORK

POOR JENNY — LIZA WEEPING

SHAGGY STORIES BY A HARRY DOG

QUEENS

The best way to get to know someone is to put yourself in their shoes—and here is your chance to do just that with the three greatest Queens in history. Follow our instructions carefully and these mighty monarchs will live as they have never lived before.

QUEEN BOACONSTRICTA

You remember Queen Boaconstricta: the Olde Englishe One with the horns sticking out of her helmet and razors out of her back axle. In fact her chariot was the original "Chopper"—so called because it made mincemeat of the Romans. The best place to stage Boaconstricta's comeback is in a traffic jam in the High Street.

What you'll need: an Olde Englishe Costume, first of all. Boaconstricta lived in the days when England wasn't England so much as Wessex, Mercedes, Throthwash and Eggstuff—ruled over by kings called Eggflip and Hrathvinegar and attacked by Vikings, Romans, Wolves and Wild Boar.

87

WOAD

Anyway, Boaconstricta wore WOAD, which was a sort of blue bodypaint. Follow her example—but since the weather's colder nowadays, fling a few animals-skins over your shoulders (preferably Prehistoric animals such as Thermolactyls).

Then sharpen your chariot-wheels and the axle-blades (an ordinary pencil-sharpener will do), put on your horned helmet and there you are—you have made history come alive again.

QUEEN ELIZABETH I

To recreate the magic and the majesty of Elizabeth I, get a red wig, stride up and down in a farthingale (that's a big hooped skirt and a very tight bodice) and say, "I may have the body of a weak and feeble woman, but this farthingale's killing me!"

Then you spy the Spanish Armadillo coming up the Channel (a bit like the Loch Ness Monster but armour-plated) and **run like mad**. Sir Walter Raleigh will throw down his cloak for you (and maybe even lend you his bicycle). And Sir Francis Drake will say, "Don't worry, ducks." So you'll be all right.

QUEEN VICTORIA

This great monarch, who was named after London's largest railway station, was known to her subjects as Victoria Sponge Fingers because of her limp handshake. To bring her to life again all you need do is dress up in deepest black, put a doily on your head, roll around on a skateboard under your six petticoats, and say, "We **are** amused!"

RIDDLES

If you thought our Ancient Jokes were old and awful and our Jokes older and worse, just wait till you've finished reading our riddles...

What's another name for a silly monkey?
A chumpanzee.

Why do heroes wear big shoes?
Because of their great feats.

When is a bus not a bus?
When it turns into a street.

Why is an empty purse always the same?
Because there's never any change in it.

Which trees do hands grow on?
Palm trees.

Where does August come before July?

In the dictionary.

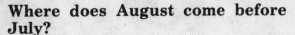

Which fish go to heaven when they die?

Angel fish.

Why was the farmer cross?

Because someone walked on his corn.

What two animals go with you everywhere?

Your calves.

What country is useful at meal-times?

China.

When is a door not a door?

When it's ajar.

Why is a fruit cake like the ocean?

Because it is full of currents.

What comes down but never goes up?
The rain.

How do you get into a locked cemetery at night?
Use a skeleton key.

What word is always pronounced Wrong?
Wrong.

What time of day was Adam created?
A little before Eve.

When is a river like the letter T?
When it must be crossed.

Why did the woodman spare the tree?
Because he was a good feller.

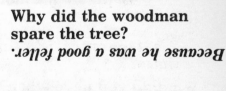

What is it that stays hot in the fridge?
Mustard.

Why does a lion have a fur coat?
It would look silly in a raincoat.

What goes up when the rain comes down?
An umbrella.

What is it that falls but never gets hurt?
Snow.

Who always goes to bed with his shoes on?
A horse.

What tables can you eat?
Vegetables.

Why do cow's wear cowbells?
Because their horns don't work.

What gets wetter the more it dries?
A towel.

What do you have when it rains beer?
An ale storm.

What is sweet, sour and violent?
Take-away Kung Food.

94

What begins with P, ends in E and
has thousands of letters?
A Post Office.

How can you make a pound note
worth more?
*Fold it and it doubles, and when you
open it again you find it in-creases.*

Why do birds fly south in
winter?
Because it's too far to walk.

How can you tell if a train has gone
past?
By the tracks it leaves.

What gets bigger the more you take
away from it?
A hole.

Why is a tall person lazier than a
short one?
Because he is longer in bed.

What did the cannibal have for
supper?
Baked beings on toast.

What should you do if you split your sides laughing?

Run until you get a stitch in them.

What animal can fly higher than a house?

All of them. Houses can't fly.

What is worse than raining cats and dogs?

Hailing buses.

How do you revive a rodent that falls in a lake?

Mouse to mouse resuscitation.

Where were English Kings usually crowned?
On the head.

What's better than a talking dog?
A spelling bee.

What kind of cat do you find in a library?
A cat-alogue.

What is a prickly pear?
Two porcupines.

Why did the boy wear two suits to the fancy dress party?
Because he went as twins.

What is a volcano?
A mountain with hiccups.

What part of an apple is the left side?
The side that isn't eaten.

What are the three easiest ways to spread gossip?
Telegraph, telephone and tell a girl.

What person always falls down on the job?
A paratrooper.

What insect does a blacksmith make?
A firefly.

Why is a dictionary dangerous?
Because it has 'dynamite' in it.

What do people do in a clock factory?
Make faces all day.

What did the boots say to the cowboy?
You ride, I'll go on foot.

What dog is religious?
A prairie dog.

How can you make seven even?
Take away the letter S.

What has teeth but no mouth?
A comb.

When is a black dog not a black dog?
When it's a grey-hound.

When is a tap not a tap?
When it's dripping.

Why couldn't the bycycle stand up?
Because it was too tyred.

SPORTS

The **Crazy Encyclopaedia** is pleased to introduce to you three of the oldest of our traditional sports. The rules and regulations set out here are in strict accordance with the guidelines set out by the International Olympic Federation.

HURLING THE STUFFED MONKEY

Stuffed monkeys are rather hard to come by, so you might have to try toy ones, especially to practise with. Hurling the Stuffed Monkey is a Victorian sport—organ-grinders used to be very good at it. But nowadays barrel organs are pretty rare too and people have had to start grinding coffee beans, their teeth, etc., instead. So the old sport of monkey-hurling is dying out.

The monkey-hurler should stand inside a circle, preferably drawn with Indian ink on a priceless carpet or picked out in huge stones and engine oil on a bowling green. Take the monkey by his tail, swing him round your head three times, and let go.

(NB: Intermediate Hurlers should wear a blindfold. At Olympic level, both hurler and monkey are blindfold. The sport is most impressive when all the spectators are blindfold, too.)

CUDDLING THE CACTUS

This was a favourite sport in America in the old days when Men were Men. In those days

it used to be called Rawhide, and the old
Pioneers used to train for weeks for a cactus-
cuddling contest with bunches of stinging
nettles to harden their flesh.

Nowadays, of course, we're all so feeble that
the rules have to be changed slightly. Instead of being stripped to the waist, the
Cuddler is allowed to wear a protective garment (a string vest). Bracing himself for the
shock, he approaches the cactus with open
arms and hugs it manfully (and painfully).
The cactus usually slaps him on the face
and says, "Have we been **introduced**?"

(NB: The Old English forms of this sport,
which have been traced in manuscripts, are
Hugging the Holly and Grasping the Nettle,
which is still found today in some areas.)

STRANGLING THE SAUSAGE

In the days of Old Queen Boaconstricta,
when both boaconstrictors and feather boas
were very common, the Anglo-Saxons used
to have a sport called Snake-Strangling.
People would volunteer to be strangled by
a snake. But gradually the sport died out,
or rather the people died, shortly followed
by the snakes, who died of boredom. Lately,
however, the sport has been revived as
Strangling the Sausage.

(NB: The National Society for Prevention of Cruelty to Sausages have made the sport more humane in recent years. Nowadays, most sausages are made entirely of sawdust, which is much kinder.)

TWERPSICHORE

Twerpsichore is what the Ancient Greeks used to call their dancing and it is still the correct term for all sorts of different dances. If you are interested in the art of twerpsichore—and are anxious to make a twerp of yourself—read on.

MORRIS DANCING

Morris dancers are part of the Rich Folk Tradition of England. To be a Morris dancer, first strap some bells around your knees. Any old bells will do: church bells, bicycle bells, hare bells. If your knees won't keep still, strap 'em together. Then it'll be more of a challenge when you come to the dancing.

You'll also need some Union Jack braces, a straw hat with ribbon tied to it, and a pig's bladder blown up like a balloon (ask the pig first!) Then all you need is some Olde English Country Music, such as:

THE GREAT SNORING NUTTING SONG

> When we did go a-nutting my lad
> When other lads were anglin'
> I spat my nut at old Bert Snort
> And it hit him on the ganglion.
> With a hey fa la ... did you ever see
> Such a queer collections of nuts as
> we.

While this is being played on the Dorset dronepipe and the Suffolk Suffolkater (a dangerous old wind instrument, usually played by Old Tom Dangleweed, another dangerous old Wind instrument) all you have to do is prance about and hit people over the head with the pig's bladder.

DISCO DANCING

What you need most of all is a large quantity of vaseline. So...grease your shoes. And your hair. And your trousers. By now you'll be a shining example to us all.

Stroll off to the Saturday Night Disco, (sliding slightly at every step) and when you arrive there, sweep the floor with your eyes.

Then, when you hear a famous Squeegees number, or maybe a song by Donna Stunner, stride masterfully out into the centre of the floor, fix the nearest group of people with your burning gaze, kick you left leg high in the air, and ... you'll bring the house down ...

BALLET

The greatest form of dancing, of course, is ballet. To be a really **great** ballet dancer you have to be called names like Anna Dabitoff or Rudolf Waterski. You also need a pair of points. If you can't find any at your local shoe shop, try British Rail. If you're a girl, you'll need a tutu. And since this is the age of equal opportunity, there's no reason why a boy shouldn't have a tututoo.

Dancers do most of their exercises at the bar, but since you're not allowed inside bars till you're sixteen, you could do yours at the sink instead. That's the origin of tap-dancing.

You'll soon learn all the positions and their lovely names, entrechats, entrechiens, tutu en l'air, tutu en shreds, pieds en l'air, pieds round le neck. Then you'll be ready for your starring role in Swan Lake...as one of the Toads.

FLYING CUPS AND SAUCERS

U.F.O.s

With the coming of the twenty-first century, yesterday's Science Fiction is rapidly turning into today's Science Fact. If you want to get in on the Interplanetary Act, the **Crazy Encyclopaedia** is happy to be of assistance.

1. **HOW TO MAKE AN UNIDENTIFIED FLYING OBJECT APPEAR IN YOUR BACK GARDEN**
Throw an elephant out of the window.

2. **HOW TO MAKE A UFO WITH FLASHING LIGHTS APPEAR IN YOUR BACK GARDEN**
Wrap the elephant up in the fairy lights from the Christmas Tree, first.

3. HOW TO TRAIN AS AN ASTRONAUT

Practise walking on the ceiling (or take it in easy stages and walk on the wall, first)

Eat all your meals out of toothpaste tubes (if you have trouble getting Roast Beef and two veg into the toothpaste tube—well, there's always semolina.)

Remember: The Moon is dead, dark, and covered with dust and craters. So get yourself into the right mood by staring at the school playing-field.

4. BEING AN ASTRONAUT'S OKAY BUT BEING AN ALIEN IS OUT OF THIS WORLD

Being an alien is the best thing of all. It's more fun! You can have pointy ears and long purple tentacles and laser beams eyesight. And maybe you could vapourise unpleasant things—such as Great Aunt Alice's bedsocks just by looking at them. So be an alien, a nice alien from somewhere like Venus—misty, silvery, gentle, and probably suffering just a little from metal fatigue. He'd look quite like us, so just spray an old shirt with silver paint, put on a pair of lurex tights and wear a colander on your head.

Then drift along to the supermarket and
make conversation with the earthlings.

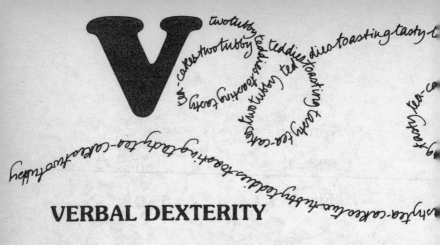

VERBAL DEXTERITY

No encyclopaedia would be complete without a guide to verbal dexterity. Since we don't want you to think that this one **is** complete (otherwise you wouldn't buy Volume Two), we are not going to give you a guide to verbal dexterity at all. Instead, we are going to **test** your verbal dexterity by giving you the world's fifty most difficult **tongue twisters** which you have got to recite out loud and faultlessly in under one minute. That's more than a second for each tongue twister, so there's no need to rush at it. Good luck!

1. Two tubby teddies toasting tasty tea-cakes.

2. A yellow yo-yo young Herbert used to use.

3. Three thrice-freed thieves.

4. They threw three thick things.

5. Flee from fog to fight 'flu fast.

6. Dressed in drip-dry drawers.

7. Deeply dreadful dreams

8. Please Paul, pause for applause.

9. Fresh fried flesh of fowl.

10. Three free flow pipes.

11. Nine nimble noblemen nibbling nuts.

12. How Harry hates hounding hares.

13. I'm anti Auntie!

14. The big black-backed bumblebee.

15. Can a canner can-can.

16. The fish-and-chip shop's chips are soft chips.

17. A laurel-crowned clown.

18. The cox crew rowed at cock's crow.

19. Charlie chooses cheese and cherries.

20. Elevating eleven elephants.

21. Fetch fifty-five foils.

22. The horses hard hoofs
hit the hard high road.

23. Georgie's gorge is gorgeous.

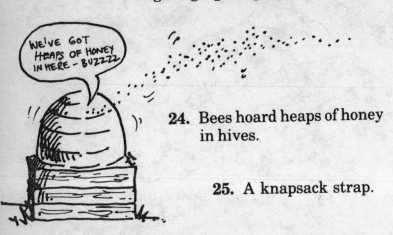

24. Bees hoard heaps of honey in hives.

25. A knapsack strap.

26. Can Kitty cuddle Clara's kitten?

27. Red leather, yellow leather.

28. Lame lambs limp.

29. Elizabeth lisps lengthy lessons.

30. The myth of Miss Muffet.

31. Don't miss the mass maths lesson.

32. One old owl occupies an old oak.

33. Tiny orangutang tongues.

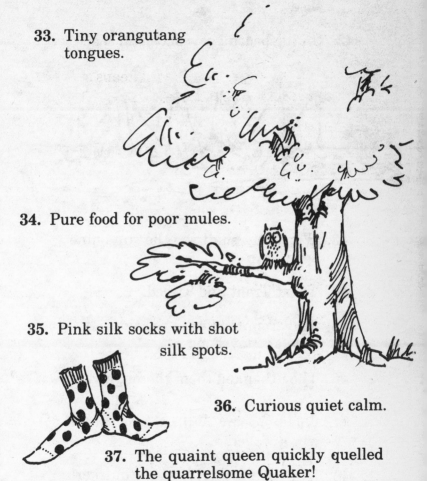

34. Pure food for poor mules.

35. Pink silk socks with shot silk spots.

36. Curious quiet calm.

37. The quaint queen quickly quelled the quarrelsome Quaker!

38. Miss Ruth's red roof thatch.

39. Rita relishes Russian radishes.

40. The sixth sheik's sixth sheep's sick.

41. She says she shall never sew a sheet.

42. On the beach I saw six small seals.

43. We surely shall see the sun shine soon.

44. Twixt Trent and Tweed.

45. Tiny Tom toddles to the tiny toddlers' toyshop.

46. They thanked them thoroughly.

47. Wishy washy Wilfred wished to win a wager.

48. Kiss her quickly! Kiss her quicker!

49. Cross crossings cautiously.

50. Thin sticks, thick bricks.

WITCHES AND WIZARDS

The jokes we began with were ancient. The ones we are ending with are **monstrous** in every sense of the word!

If a flying saucer is an aircraft, what is a flying broom?
Witchcraft.

What dance do vampires do?
The Fang-dango.

119

What do you call a witch trying to thumb a lift?

A witch-hiker.

Why do little witches get A's in school?

Because they are good at spell-ing.

What skeleton was once emperor of France?

Napoleon Bones-apart.

What happens if you don't pay the exorcist?

You get re-possessed.

Why didn't the skeleton cross the road?
Because he didn't have the guts.

What did the ghost say to the barman?
Do you serve spirits here?

Which Monster is unlucky?
The Luck Less Monster.

Did you hear about the witch who couldn't write a decent letter?
She couldn't spell properly.

Why does a witch ride on a broom?
Because a vacuum cleaner is too heavy.

GEE-UP

What do you call a wicked old woman who lives by the sea?
A sand-witch.

What do short-sighted ghosts wear?
Spooktacles.

How does a witch tell the time?
By her witch-watch.

Witch in hospital: 'Doctor, I feel much better now'.
Doctor: 'Good, you can get up for a spell this afternoon'.

What do ghosts take for a bad cold?
Coffin drops.

What do ghosts eat for breakfast?
Dreaded wheat.

What does a polite vampire say?
Fang you very much.

Why do ghosts always lie perfectly flat when they are asleep?
Because they use a spirit level.

Why do devils and ghosts get on so well together?
Because demons are a ghoul's best friend.

Where does a vampire save his money?
At the blood bank.

What's it called when demons show off?
A demon-stration.

123

PHANTOMIME

What sort of show do ghosts like the best?
Phantomimes.

What kind of ship was Dracula captain of?
A blood vessel.

What spirit was a great painter?
Vincent Van Ghost.

Why did the monster have to go into hospital?
To have his ghoul stones removed.

What game did Dr. Jekyll like to play best?
Hyde and Seek.

What do you call a monster who comes down your chimney at Christmas?

Santa Claus.

Why did the witch take her broomstick to bed?

Because she didn't want to walk in her sleep.

Is a drunken ghost a methylated spirit?

Why Did Frankenstein give up boxing?

Because he didn't want to spoil his looks.

What do you call a vampire's son?

A bat boy.

Where does Frankenstein's wife have her hair done?

At the ugly parlour.

What game do ghost children play?

Haunt and seek.

How do witches drink tea?
With cups and sorcerers.

What kind of music does a ghost like?
Haunting melodies.

How can you tell twin witches apart?
Well, it's not easy to tell witch is which.

What did the mother ghost say to the child ghost?
Don't spook until you're spooken to.

XYZ

It's time to make an eXit.

Y?

Because ZiZ iZ Ze end!

Let's go out with a bang...

DAFT
DICTIONARY

ACORN

an oak in a nutshell

AUTOGRAPH

a chart showing the sales figures of cars

ATTACK

a small nail

AUCTIONEER

a man who looks
forbidding

ASHTRAY

a place where people
put out their cigar-
ettes when the room
doesn't have a carpet

ARREST

something you take
when you're tired

APRICOTS

beds for baby
monkeys

6

APPEAR

something you fish off

ANNOUNCE

one-sixteenth of a
pound

ACTOR

a man who tries to be
everything but him-
self

ADULT

a person who has
stopped growing at
both ends and started
growing in the middle

7

ADVERTISING

makes you think
you've longed all
your life for some-
thing when you've
never even heard of it

ATOM

a male pussy cat

ABYSS

an Abbot's wife

AUTOBIOGRAPHY

a car's log book

8

APEX

a female gorilla

ANTELOPE

when two insects run off to get married without their parents knowing

ANTI-FREEZE

a female relative from Iceland

ANTIBODY

uncle's fat wife

ASTRONOMER

a night watchman

ARCHEOLOGIST

a man whose career lies in ruins

ATOMIC BOMB

something that makes molehills out of mountains

ALARM CLOCK

something to scare the daylight **into** you

ABUNDANCE

222 dancing cakes

ARMIES

the things you've got
up your sleevies

AREA CODE

a cold that hits one
part of the country at
a time

AFFORD

a car some people
drive

BACTERIA

the rear of a cafeteria

BEETROOT

a potato with very
high blood pressure

BEE

a hum-bug

12

BATHING BEAUTY

a girl worth wading for

BARBER'S SHOP

a clip joint

BOYCOTT

a small bed that's no good for girls

BUTTRESS

a dairy maid who makes butter

BULLETIN

a can of corned beef

BALLYHOO

a directory of well-known ballet dancers correctly called *The Ballyhoo's Hoo*

BLUBBER

weeping and whaling

BLAZER

a fire that looks like a jacket

BELLICOSE

a warm, fat stomach

BASHFUL

a retired boxer

BAREFACED

looking like a bear

BARBARIAN

the man who cuts
your hair badly

BLUNDERBUSS

a vehicle that goes
from Edinburgh to
Glasgow taking a
short cut via London

BRUSSELS SPROUT

an ornamental foun-
tain in the Belgian
capital

BOXER

a fellow who stands
up for the other
fellow's rights

BORE

someone who wants
to tell you about
himself when you
want to tell him
about yourself

BIGAMIST

someone who makes
the same mistake
twice

BUNIONS

what you get when
you cross a rabbit
with a leek

BULLDOZER

a sleeping bull

CANNIBAL

someone who is fed up with people

CHAIR

headquarters for hindquarters

CARTOON

a song you sing in the car

CATERPILLAR

an upholstered worm

COMMENTATOR

a talking spud

CONCEIT

I-strain

CROWBAR

a drinking place for crows

CAMELOT

a herd of dromedaries

CARBUNCLE

an automobile with a dent in it

COINCIDE

the sensible thing to do when it's raining

CABBAGE

the age of a taxi

CONFERENCE

a meeting of the bored

CACTUS

an overgrown pin cushion

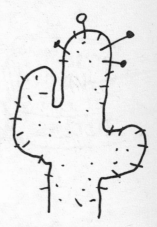

CARNATION

a country where everyone owns a car

CHARCOAL

what the cleaning lady puts into the fire

CATACOMB

what goes with the
cat's brush

CARAMEL

a motorised camel

CATASTROPHE

the prize awarded to
the top pussy at the
cat show

COWARD

a man who thinks
with his legs

CLIMATE

the only thing you
can do with a ladder

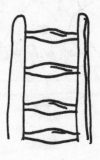

CAULIFLOWER

the blossom a dog
wears in his button
hole

COMMITTEE

a body that keeps
minutes and wastes
hours

CRIMINAL

one who gets caught

23

CHAMPAGNE

the French for 'false window'

CROSSROADS

angry motorways

CLOAK

the sound made by a Chinese frog

CAMEL

a warped horse

COCOON

a wound-up
caterpillar

CHIPMUNK

a French friar

CELLMATES

two germs living
together

CARPET

material bought by
the yard and worn
out by the foot

CRANE

a bird trained to lift
extremely heavy
weights

DENIAL

where Cleopatra
lived

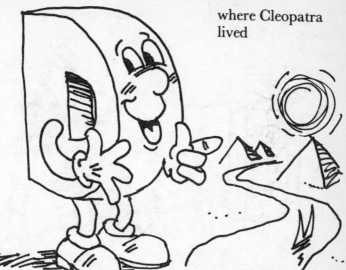

DENTIST

someone who always
looks down in the
mouth

DRILL SERGEANT

an army dentist

DEPTH

height turned upside down

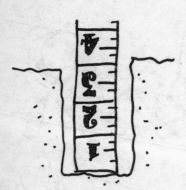

DULCET

a boring tennis match

DIATRIBE

an extinct race

DOLDRUMS

percussion instruments played by girls

DRAWING ROOM

where a dentist works

DIAGRAM

a record player that's broken

DURATION

an oration that never stops

DISCONSOLATE

a record being played after midnight

29

DACHSHUND

half a dog high by a
dog and a half long

DIPLOMAT

one who thinks twice
before saying nothing

EXPERIENCE

what people call their
mistakes

EPITAPH

a statement that lies
above about the per-
son that lies below

ECHO

the only thing that
can't stop you getting
the last word

HEAR
LIES

ECHO POINT

31

ELECTRICIAN

a switch doctor

EARWIG

a piece of false hair
worn over the ears

EROS

brave people

EQUINOX

strange tapping
noises usually heard
in haunted houses
after dark

EXPERT

someone who used to
be a Pert

ERASER

what the artist's wife
said when she saw
him drawing a nude

ENGLISH CHANNEL

a British television
station

EXTINCT

a dead skunk

EVE

what you shout at the
start of a tug-o'-war

ELLIPTICAL

a kiss from a man
with a moustache

FLOOD

a river that's too big
for its bridges

FRUSTRATE

in the top class

FORTUNE

a singing quartet

35

FARTHINGALE

a cheap hurricane

FACTORY

a set of encyclopaedias

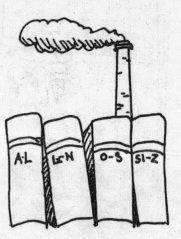

FASTIDIOUS

someone who is quick
and ugly

FUGUE

a thick fog

FAUCET

what you have to do
when the door is
jammed

FIDDLESTICK

something you use to
play the violin

FLEECE

insects that get into your
wool if you don't
wash regularly

FIGMENT

what Adam and Eve
wore in the Garden
of Eden

FLATTERY

a battery that's run
out of power

FRIEND

someone who has the
same enemies as you

FJORD

a Norwegian motor
car

FORUM

Two-um plus two-um

GALLOWS

where no noose is
good noose

GOSSIP

letting the chat out of
the bag

GOBLET

a small turkey

GANGRENE

a group of Martians

GALLERY

a home for girls

GRANARY

a home for grannies

GONDOLIER

when you've wiped
the grin off your face

GENERALLY

an Arab general

HUMBUG

a musical insect

HAIR TONIC

medicine for rabbits

HATCHET

what a hen does to an egg

42

HYACINTH

what you say when
you first meet Lady
Cynthia

HERMIT

a lady's glove

HAY

high-class grass

HOGWASH

a pig's laundry

HACKNEYED

the opposite of knock-kneed

HYPOCHONDRIAC

a person with an infinite capacity for faking pains

HATLESS

the strong man who carried the world on his shoulders

HONESTY

fear of getting caught

HOSPITALS

places where people
who are run down
wind up

HUG

a roundabout way of
expressing affection

HYPOCRITE

a man who sets a
good example when
other people are watch-
ing

HIPPIES

the things you hang
your leggies on

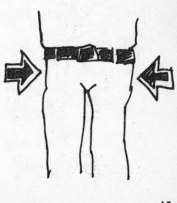

HOLIDAY

the time when you
find out where **not** to
go next year

ILLEGAL

a sick bird of prey

IGLOO

an icicle made for two

ICED LOLLY

Eskimo money

IGNORANCE

when you don't know
something and
somebody finds out

IRONY

the instrument used
for pressing clothes
on an ironing board

IDOLISE

lazy eyeballs

INCOME

you try to make it
first, then you try to
make it last

IMPIOUS

a religious elf

IMPALE

white-faced Red
Indian

INKLING

a very small pen

INTENSE

a camping holiday

ICE

skid stuff

INCONGRUOUS

where American laws
are made

INFORMATION

how planes fly at an
air show

INDISTINCT

where the dirty dishes
go

ICEBERG

a kind of permanent
wave

ICICLE

an eavesdropper

IMPASSABLE

a slippery football

ICE CREAM

but only when I'm
frightened

IMPROVEMENT

a guest who is always
welcome to stay, as in
'There's always room
for improvement'

JUMP

the last word in aeroplanes

JAYWALKING

a hobby that gives you that run-down feeling

JODHPURS

the noise made by two happy cats

JUGULAR

shaped like a Grecian urn

JOKE

something not every-body gets

KIDNEY

the knee of a baby goat

KNOB

a thing to adore

KINDRED

a fear of being visited by relatives

55

LETTUCE SALAD

correspondence you
can eat

LEOPARD

a dotted lion, as in 'to
open this packet tear
along dotted lion'

LITHE

falsehoods told by
someone who lisps

LATTICE

a green window
much liked by rabbits

LOBSTER

a tennis player

LOGARITHMS

wooden dance tunes

LOST CHORD

something you look for
when playing Haydn
seek (after you've been
to the shops with your
Chopin Liszt)

LAUNDRY

a place where clothes
are mangled

LUXURY

something that costs
£5 to make and £105
to sell

LUCK

when a man picks up
a horse-shoe on the
road, and is knocked
by a car into a field of
four-leaf clovers as a
black cat walks by

LIGHT SLEEPER

someone who goes to
bed in a chandelier

LYRE

a dishonest harp

MINIMUM

Minidad's wife

MITTENS

what you get when a cat swallows a ball of wool

MONEY

the Royal Mint makes it first and you try to make it last

MONOLOGUE

an unmarried piece
of wood

MALADY

a duchess

MELANCHOLY

a dogs that likes
melons

MUSHROOM

the place where they
cook school dinners

MUMMY

an Egyptian pressed
for time

MOTEL

William Tell's sister

MISTLETOE

astronaut's athlete's
foot

MAGPIE

a pudding made with
old magazines

MARGIN

mummy's favourite
tonic

MOUNTEBANK

the place where the
Canadian police keep
their money

MOSQUITO

a flying hypodermic
needle

MOUNTAIN RANGE

a cooker made
specially for use at
high altitudes

MOUNTAIN CLIMBER

a man who always wants to take one more peak

MACARONI

the inventor of the wireless who used his noodle and pasta message through spaghetti

MINCE

white sweet with a hole in the middle and a peppermint flavour

MERMAID

a creature that's half a girl and half a sardine

METER

a butcher with a car

MACAROON

a famous Scots biscuit

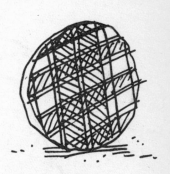

MISFIRED

a secretary who has
been given the sack

MUSTARD

the only thing that
stays hot in the fridge

FROZEN
MUSTARD

MULTIPLICATION
TABLE

the longest table in
the world

NUMBER

the first thing to take
when you're run
down

NUDIST CAMP

a place where hardly
anything goes on

NORTH POLE

someone who comes
from Warsaw

NECTAR

a garment worn
round the neck

NIGHTINGALE

an evening out in a
storm

NAIL

a long thin pointed
object with a flat
head which you aim
at while hitting your
thumb with a
hammer

NUDIST

someone who goes
around without a
vest, a shirt or a
jacket and wears
trousers to match

MATCHING WARDROBE

OBESITY

surplus gone to waist

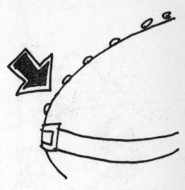

OPPORTUNIST

someone who meets a
wolf at the door and
the next day appears
wearing a fur coat

OPTIMISM

the cheerful spirit
that makes it possible
for a kettle to whistle
with boiling water up
its nose

OPERETTA

the person who answers when you dial 100 on the telephone

OUT OF BOUNDS

an exhausted kangaroo

OTTOMAN

a car mechanic

OPTIMIST

a hope addict

OYSTER

what you shout when
you want someone to
lift up your mother

OCTOPUS

a cat with eight feet

OBOE

a tramp

ODIOUS

poetry that stinks

OBLIQUE

time to call in the plumber

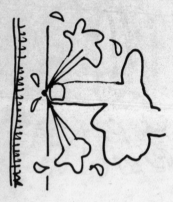

OMELETTE

Prince of Denmark, a play by William Shakespeare rich in fowl play and eggsitement

POLYGON

a dead parrot

PRICKLY PEAR

two hedgehogs

PINE

what sad fir trees do

PANTS

what trousers do on a
long run up a steep
hill

PACIFIST

someone who punches
you on the nose
peacefully

PRUNE

a plum that's seen
better days

POLYGAMIST

a parrot with more
than one wife

PAINFUL

a glass house
(Please remember
that people who live
in glass houses should
undress in the
basement)

PHONOGRAPH

a chart used by the
Post Office to record
telephone sales

PALAVER

a kind of sweater

PHARMACY

the science of
agriculture

PARKING SPACE

always filled with
somebody else's car

PAVEMENT ARTIST

someone who draws
pictures on his knees

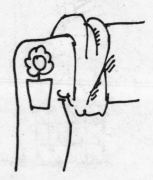

PARADOX

two doctors

PSYCHIATRIST

someone who doesn't
have to worry as long
as other people do

PARATROOPER

an Army drop-out

PHYSICIST

a man who makes
ginger beer

PEA

a vegeta-pill

POULTRY

a tree that chickens
like roosting in

PUTTY

miniature golf

PIGEON-TOED

half-pigeon, half-toad

PROPAGANDA

a well-behaved and
upper-class goose

PRINTER

a man of letters

POSSE

a cat from the Wild
West

POPULACE

frilly material that
people like

PROFESSOR

a textbook wired for
sound

POLITICS

a parrot that's
swallowed a watch

PASTEURISE

too far to see

PYRAMID

an organised pile of
Egyptian rocks

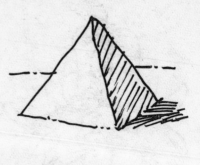

PARACHUTE

a double-barrelled
shotgun

PARTY

Dad's supper

PUPILS

what a cross-eyed
teacher can't control

PEN FRIENDS

pigs that get on well
together

PORCUPINE

an unhappy slice of
bacon

PYGMY

a tiny pig (Shakespeare
wrote about one in his
play *Hamlet*)

PRAWN

one of the small pieces used in the game of Chess

PILLOW

headquarters

PICKLE

a cucumber in a spot of bother

PORTABLE

a cheap piece of furniture to eat off

PANTRY

the room where you
keep your underwear

PIPECLEANER

a toothpick wearing
long woolly under-
wear

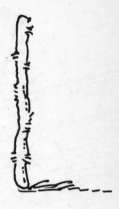

Q
a long line that
people stand in

QUACK

a duck's doctor

QUAKER

a nervous lady

84

QUICKSAND

the reason the hour-
glass is ten minutes'
fast

QUADRUPLETS

four crying out loud!

QUINCE

five children at one
time

QUATRAIN

a railway train with
four carriages

RUBBER BAND

see
STRING QUARTET

RUNNER BEANS

special food for
athletes

RINGLEADER

the first one in the
bath

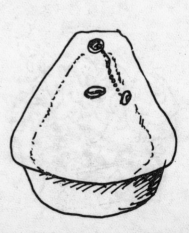

RAZOR

an alarm clock for girls

RECITED

going back to take a second look

RESEARCH

looking for something twice

RUBBER GLOVES

things you put on when you want to wash your hands without getting them wet

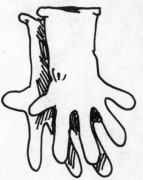

RAISIN

a very old and very
anxious grape

RECLUSE

a Chinaman going on
his second cruise

REBATE

putting another
worm onto the hook

ROMANCE

ants in Rome

RAWHIDE

a nudist's clothes

RUGGED

feeling tough when you're sitting on the carpet

REORIENTATE

a Chinaman return-ing to China

RANSOM

a four-minute miler

RHUBARB

bloodshot celery

RAGAMUFFIN

a toasted teacake
made from old
clothes

ROTUNDA

an author's pen
name, as in 'Samuel
Clemens rotunda the
name Mark Twain'

REPARTEE

the second party
you've been to this
week

SAGO

how you start a
pudding race

SIGNATURE

a baby swan's
autograph

STRING QUARTET

see
RUBBER BAND

SEE-SAW

what you use to cut
through giant waves

SEA SHELLS

what you fire from
underwater guns

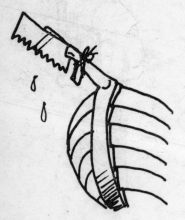

SINGING

your bathright

SECRET

something you tell
everybody one by
one

SANDWICH

an attempt to make
both ends meat

SCULPTOR

someone who makes
faces

SELF-CONTROL

someone who can
open a bag of peanuts
and eat just one

SYNONYM

a word you use in
place of one you can't
spell

SNOW

well-dressed rain

SAGE

a man who knows his
onions

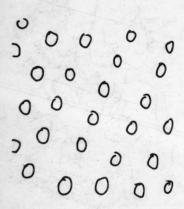

SPELLBOUND

the way a dictionary
is covered

STABILISED

a horse that's locked
in and can't get out

SONATA

Mr. and Mrs. Ata's
eldest boy

SCRAPBOOK

a boxer's diary

SHAMROCK

a phoney rock

SHAMPOO

a phoney smell

SNUFF

no more, as in 'That's
snuff, thank you, I'm
full up'

SOMERSAULT

what goes with
pepper from May
to September

SHOTGUN

an exhausted gun

SLEEPING BAG

a nap sack

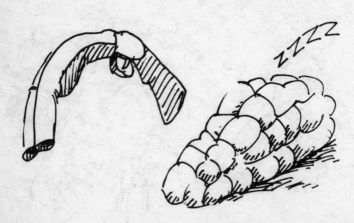

SQUARE ROOT

a diced turnip

SNORING

sheet music

SKELETON

a guy inside out with
his outside off

SUSPICIOUS SOUNDING

an elephant hanging
over the edge of a
cliff with its tail tied
to a daisy

SICK REPTILE

an illigator

SCALES

the part of a fish that
weighs the most

SPRINGTIME

the moment you sit
on a drawing pin

SKINDIVER

a mosquito

98

TOMORROW

today's greatest
labour-saving
device

I'LL CUT THE GRASS TOMORROW

TRICYCLE

a tot rod

TEARS

glum drops

TROJAN HORSE

a phoney pony

TRANSPARENT

Dad or Mum in a
trance

TAXIDERMIST

a stuffed cab driver

TEMPEST

an ill-tempered little
nuisance

TYRANT

someone who gets into a temper when he can't tie his tie properly

TELEVISION

radio with eyestrain

TONGUE TWISTER

something that gets your tang tongueled

TUBE

in English it means a hollow cylinder, but in Dutch it means a silly Hollander

UNABRIDGED

a river you have to
swim across

UNDERCOVER AGENT

a spy in bed

ULTRAMARINE

the best sailor in the
entire navy

UNISON

an only boy

UNIT

a term of abuse, as in 'Can't you even spell apple correctly, unit!'

VITAMIN

what you do when
someone comes
round to see you

VESTRY

the room where you
keep your vests

VOLCANO

a mountain that's
blown its stack

VOWEL

cheating in sport, as
in 'he's definitely
guilty of vowel play'

WATCHDOG

an animal that goes 'Woof, tick, woof, tick, woof, tick'

WAITER

someone who thinks money grows on trays

WEDDING RING

a metal tourniquet worn on the left hand to stop circulation

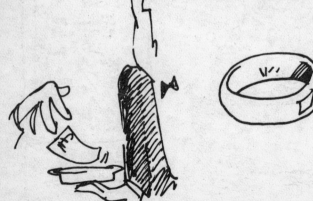

WHOLESOME

the only thing in the world you can take whole and still have some left

WALKIE-TALKIE

a parrot out for a stroll

WASHABLE

giving a bath to a bull

WATER

thirst-aid

WIND

air in a hurry

WINTER

twelve months in England

WINDOW SHOPPING

going out to buy new windows for the house

WHISKY

two pints of which make one cavort

WINE

the noise made by an unhappy bottle of alcohol

WOODWORM

a do-it-yourself carpenter

WIRELESS

a human puppet

WOE

the opposite of 'giddy-up'

X-RAY

bellyvision

XYLOPHONE

revolutionary
instrument invented
in 1860 by Alexander
Graham Xylo

X

what hens lay

HELLO!

YELLOW

what you do when
you stub your toe

YESMEN

the people who are
around the fellow
nobody noes

YEAR

are you listening, as
in 'D'year what I
said just now?'

ZEBRA

a horse that's escaped
from prison

ZINC

the place you wash
the zaucepans

ZUB

noise made by a bee
flying backwards

There are 72 letters in the Cambodian alphabet. Consider
yourself lucky that you got given the English edition of the
Daft Dictionary.